1. Janko Domsic
Untitled, undated (detail)
Biro and crayon on cardboard
44.5 × 34 cm
Private collection

Inner Worlds Outside

A Supplement

Whitechapel Gallery, London
28 April – 25 June 2006

Contents

Introduction

'Art does not lie down on the bed that is made for it; it runs away as soon as one says its name; it loves to be incognito. Its best moments are when it forgets what it is called.' *Jean Dubuffet*

After World War II, the French artist Jean Dubuffet became known as the leading champion of art produced outside the mainstream. Around 1940, he began to collect children's drawings before turning his attention to work by psychiatric patients, mediums, self-taught visionaries and criminal offenders amongst other so-called 'eccentric' individuals. He acquired work by many diverse artists such as Augustin Lesage, Madge Gill and Adolf Wölfli and identified shared traits in raw, spontaneous and deeply individualistic ways of working that he labelled 'Art Brut'.

Since the mid 1900s, a problematic distinction had developed between established, 'mainstream' artists and individuals producing art from the 'fringes of society'. In artistic circles, artists like Paul Klee and Pablo Picasso sought art that was spontaneous and unadulterated by knowledge in opposition to what they considered an over sophisticated and self-conscious western tradition. Expressionists like Wassily Kandinsky and Alfred Kubin prioritised intuition and spontaneity over reason and knowledge, exploring the depth of the psyche and its potential for autonomous creativity. Influenced by their theories, Hans Prinzhorn, the Austrian art historian turned psychiatrist played a crucial role in fuelling the interests of the Surrealists, who were drawn by both the childlike innocence and subconscious explorations of people the English writer Roger Cardinal was to call 'Outsider Artists'.

However, the definition of *Outsider* Art with its insistence on social isolation and an autonomous creativity devoid of external influences, is deeply problematic. Descriptions of *Outsider* Art have tended to be based on sociological and psychological factors and the artists' fundamental difference from a dominant cultural 'norm'. Increasingly this kind of categorisation has

7

seemed out of step with a postmodernist sensibility and has been redressed in recent times paralleling advances in the understanding of psychological disorders.

This publication and the exhibition it accompanies aim to explode many of the myths surrounding *Outsider* artists. They seek out the parallels between *Insider* and *Outsider* art and the impact of unknown *Outsiders* on some of the greatest names of 20th century art. The exhibition considers *Insiders* and *Outsiders* as the two sides of the same 'modernist' tendency, sharing a common discourse that connects the visual arts to social sciences, including anthropology, sociology, psychology and psychoanalysis.

A supplement to the catalogue and exhibition organised with Fundación 'La Caixa', Madrid and the Irish Museum of Modern Art, Dublin, this publication contains a number of works added for the presentation in London and includes brief biographies of the additional artists. As in the original catalogue and exhibition, the works are loosely arranged into the following sections: Imaginary Landscapes and Fantastic Cities, The Allure of Language, Faces and Masks, The Erotic Body, Fantastic Dreams and Haunting Tales. It also includes two additional sections. The first, titled Environments, provides a small snapshot of the extraordinary gardens or installations, usually the culmination of years of obsessive work, that can be found in remote corners of the world. The second is devoted to the seemingly endless outpourings of the mediumistic artist Madge Gill who lived in London's East End and claimed to be guided by a spirit called 'Myrninerest'.

The works in this publication were principally selected from three major collections of *Outsider* Art. Some of the finest examples of Henry Darger's epic narratives, Charles Dellschau's heroic flying machines and Jesse Howard's poignant sign paintings, to name only a few, were borrowed from an extraordinary anonymous private collection. Almost forty works have been borrowed from The Bethlem Royal Hospital Archives and Museum. This was established from a combination of the collections at the original 'Bedlam', one of the world's oldest hospitals for the care and treatment of people with mental health problems and the Maudsley Hospital, a postgraduate psychiatric teaching hospital. This collection specialises in work by artists who have suffered from mental health problems although there are exceptions and the pictures come from many different sources. Other works by such diverse artists as Michel Nedjar, Theo Wagemann and Adolf Wölfli, for example, were selected from over 800 works that form the Musgrave Kinley Collection of Outsider Art, which is now on long-term loan to the Irish Museum of Modern Art, Dublin. In addition, numerous works by Madge Gill were borrowed from the London Borough of Newham Heritage Services where they were donated by her family. There are also a number of works by Insiders, carefully selected either because of a sympathetic style or because they reveal *Outsider* influences in a quest for anti-rational expression. *Insiders* like Jean-Michel Basquiat, Roberto Matta and Mark Tobey are included because their interests in primal languages or symbols resulted in intense, raw or direct expressions that bear the qualities associated with *Outsider* art.

We would like to express particular thanks to our patrons and sponsors for their unstinting encouragement and support of this project, without which this publication would not have been possible. Our thanks are also extended to all the lenders for their generosity in parting, often at short notice, with their important works for this exhibition. We would also like to thank J. Michael Phillips and his colleagues at the Archives and Museum Service of the Bethlem Royal Hospital as well as Paul Pert, Sean Sherman and their colleagues at Newham Heritage Services and Eimear Martin and Catherine Marshall at The Irish Museum of Modern Art. We are also indebted to Jon Thompson for his energy and vision in forming this exhibition and publication and to Monika Kinley for her thorough involvement in every aspect of the project and her generosity in lending works. The exhibition's organiser Soledad Gutiérrez also deserves our recognition for her extraordinary efficiency and flair in co-ordinating the smooth development of this project. Our thanks also to the photographers and to O-SB Design for elegantly bringing these disparate parts together in a beautifully designed whole.

Iwona Blazwick, Director
Anthony Spira, Curator
Whitechapel Gallery

Imaginary Landscapes
and Fantastic Cities

Most artists are concerned with the shared environment either as immediate experience or as it figures in the imagination. Working on the grandest possible scale is the Chicago-based, reclusive artist Henry Darger, represented by a number of works from his epic series of 8,000 drawings depicting the conflict between the five *Vivian Girls* and the powers of darkness. In complete contrast, only two small drawings of mysterious and elegiac landscapes with satanic overtones survive from an anonymous artist from the Bethlem Royal Hospital Archives and Museum.

While Willem van Genk's *Trolleybus*, is made from found materials and deals directly with life in the city, Jean Dubuffet's earthbound *Herbages au corbeau*, 1952, depicts a real but somewhat remote place in an imaginatively enhanced form,

inspired by the discovery of prehistoric cave drawings in Lascaux in 1940. The American artist Bill Traylor often depicted schematized figures or farm animals in drawings that he hung from string on street fences to entertain and encourage an audience among the local people. Credited with painting the first modern abstract works, Wassily Kandinsky is represented here by a drawing that retains the traces of a landsacape despite his quest for spontaneous 'improvisations' based on non-representational qualities. Charles Dellschau's extraordinary flying machines are a highly inventive articulation of an age-old human impulse. They encapsulate heroic dreams that herald trans-Atlantic flights and early passenger dirigibles and have even been claimed as evidence of extraterrestrial life in the 1850s.

5. Augustin Lesage
L' Esprit de la pyramide, c. 1927
Oil on canvas
67.5 × 98 cm
Private collection

6. Jean Dubuffet
Herbages au corbeau
(Paturages au corbeau), October 1952
Oil on canvas
97.2 × 130 cm
Courtesy Waddington Galleries Ltd.

7. Wassily Kandinsky
Untitled, 1915–16
Watercolour and Indian ink
on paper laid down on board
47 × 63.5 cm
Private collection on care
of Grosvenor Gallery

8. Roberto Matta
Untitled, 1939
Crayon and graphite on paper
32.4 × 49.8 cm
J. Todd Figi, La Jolla, CA

13

9. Augustin Lesage
No 166, 1944–1945
Oil on canvas
135 × 240 cm
Private collection

10. Willem van Genk
Trolleybus, c.1995
Cardboard, found objects
Length 50 cm
Private collection

11. Bill Traylor
Untitled (Horse), c.1939–42
Pencil and poster paint
on cardboard
39 × 36 cm
Private collection

12. Eugene von Bruenchenhein
#769, c. 1958
Oil on board
61 × 61 cm
Private collection

13. Charles Dellschau
4345 Curtis Planes (recto) | 4345 If I Had the Means (verso), c. 1919
Collage, pencil and watercolour on paper
45 × 38 cm
Private collection

14. Charles Dellschau
4422 Mira (recto) | 4423 Mira (verso), c. 1919
Collage, pencil and watercolour on paper
45 × 40 cm
Private collection

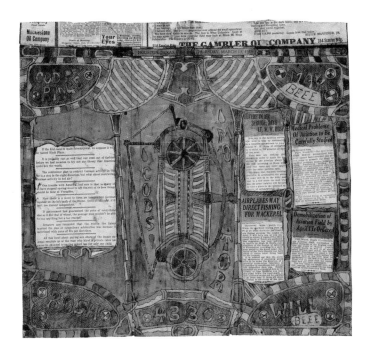
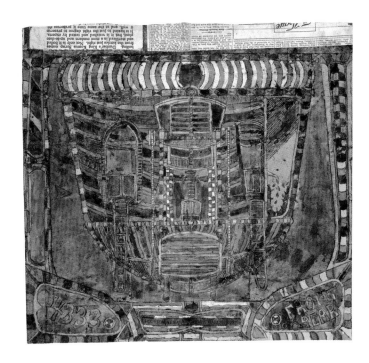

15. Charles Dellschau
4330 Cod's Motor (recto) | 4333 Front Rear (verso), c. 1919
Collage, pencil and watercolour on paper
39.5 × 42 cm
Private collection

16. Charles Dellschau
4333 Shall Be Will Be (recto) | 4334 Codridges (verso), c. 1919
Collage, pencil and watercolour on paper
47 × 41.2 cm
Private collection

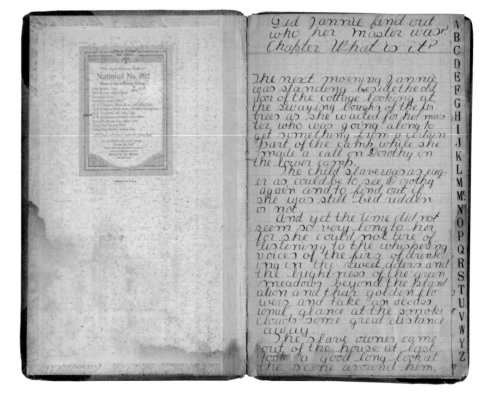

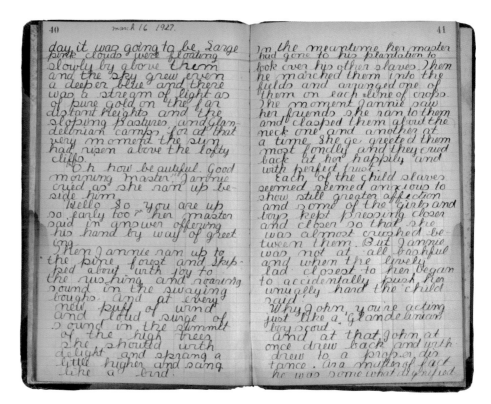

18. Henry Darger
Book, c.1927
Board and paper
32 × 20 cm
Private collection

17. Henry Darger
Untitled c.1940s–1960s
Untitled (recto)/'At ressurrectoaction run. In fright
they see a train coming sixty-five miles an hour only ten
seconds to save her'. (verso)
Carbon tracing, collage, pencil and watercolour on paper
61 × 96 cm
Private collection

19. Henry Darger
Untitled, c.1940s–1960s
199 part one. 'Captured again with rescued
children by Glandelinian boy scouts'. (verso)
Carbon tracing, collage, pencil and
watercolour on paper
60.5 × 300.6 cm
Private collection

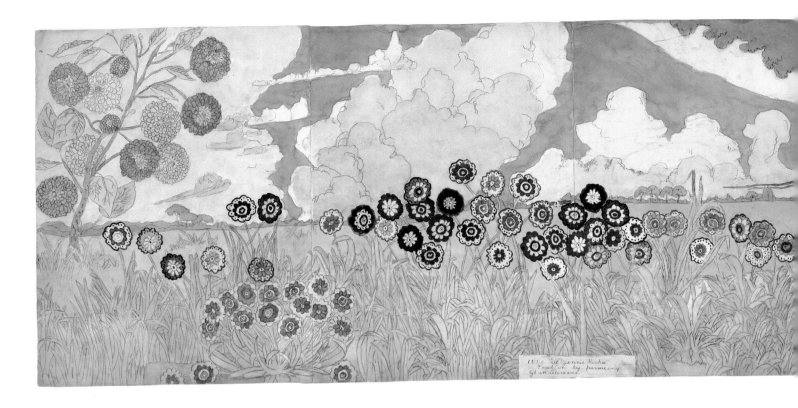

20. Henry Darger
Untitled, c.1940s–1960s
153. 'At Jennie Richee – Fired on by pursueing Glandelinians'. (recto)
154. 'At Jennie Richee – With Blengiglomenean absent for short time,
Foe take advantage and presses them hard. One soldier helps them
to no avail when they're out of bullets'. (verso)
Carbon tracing, collage, pencil and watercolour on paper
60.5 × 270.5 cm
Private collection

21. Henry Darger
Untitled, c.1940s–1960s
110. 'At Jennie Richie. Safeguard child under half destroyed shelter untill hurricane like thunderstorm slackens'. (recto)
111. 'At Jennie Richee. Frustrate enemy second time by warning Emperor Vivian during progress of storm'. (verso)
Carbon tracing, collage, pencil and watercolour on paper
58 × 271.0 cm
Private collection

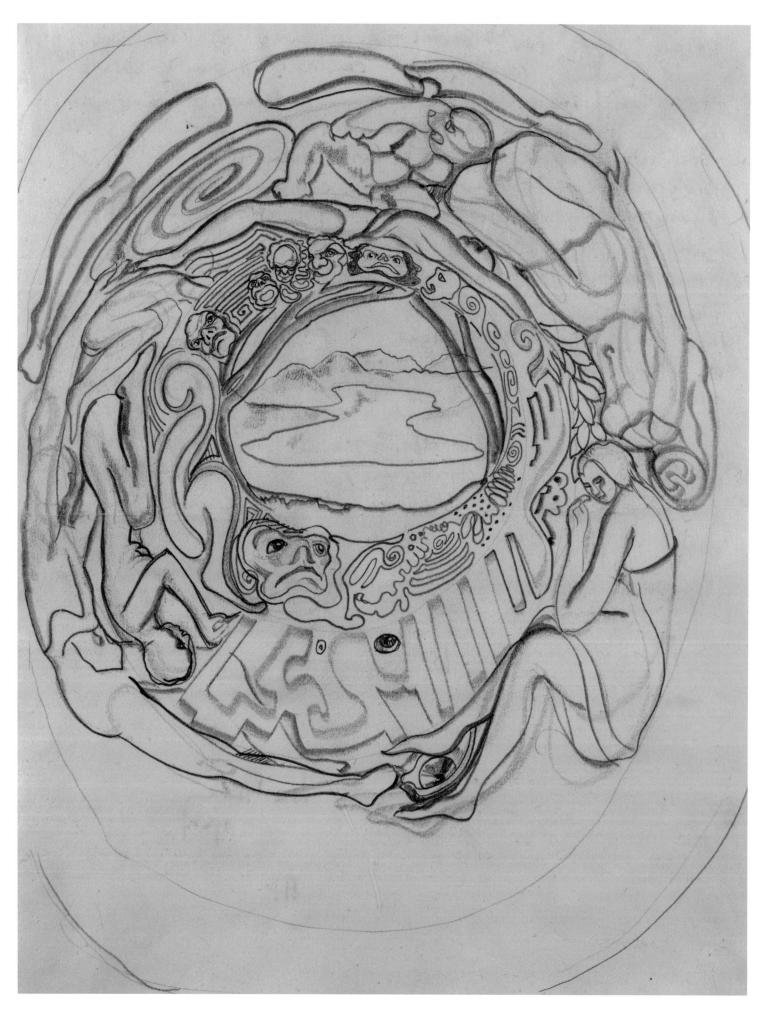

23. Anonymous
Satan and Cross, undated
Pencil on paper
12.3 × 19.9 cm
Bethlem Art and Collections Trust

24. Anonymous
Rocky Landscape, undated
Pencil on paper
12.3 × 19.9 cm
Bethlem Art and Collections Trust

22. William M.G. Murray
All Things Good or Evil, 1943
Pencil on paper
25.3 × 20.4 cm
Bethlem Art and Collections Trust

The Allure of Language

Many artists have explored written language: as document, as coded structure, alphabet design and/or inscription and this preoccupation surfaces in all sections of the exhibition. A number of works here attempt to reinvent language by devising sets of hieroglyphs and signs. Some works appear to seek out new forms of communication while others develop personal, secret signs, either based on universal languages and traditions or indulging in ornate, decorative pictograms.

This section includes an extraordinary book of written signs by James Castle who was born profoundly deaf and apparently never learnt to read or write. Mark Tobey's *Blue Interior*, 1959, is the culmination of a profound spiritual and musical enquiry and an interest in Chinese, Persian and Arabic calligraphy. Gilbert Price, whose work is from the Bethlem Royal Hospital Museum and Archives, is an artist about whom we know very little. His pictograms include ornate decorative fences as well as funnels, chimneys, vases and hand positions that conflate different sign systems in a playful pictorial game. The Belgian poet and painter Henri Michaux made a number of intricate drawings under the influence of mescaline, that he took in an attempt to escape the constraints of conventional language. Also included in this section are examples of Adolf Wölfli's restless, symmetrical drawings that form part of his fanciful autobiography. This was interspersed with poetry, musical compositions and three thousand illustrations to form a twenty-five thousand page book, hand-bound by the artist.

25. James Castle
Untitled Book, undated
Found paper, string and soot
17 × 16.5 cm
Private collection

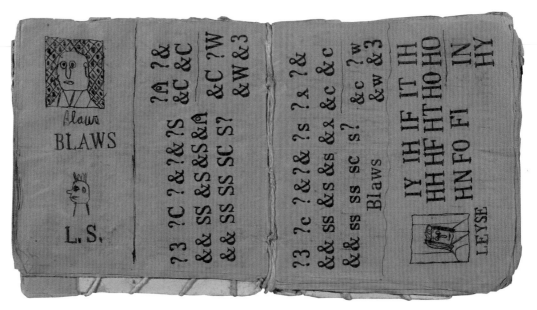

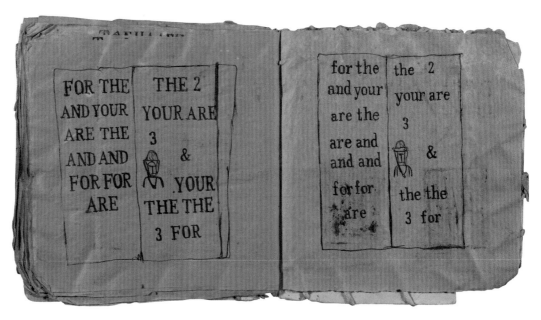

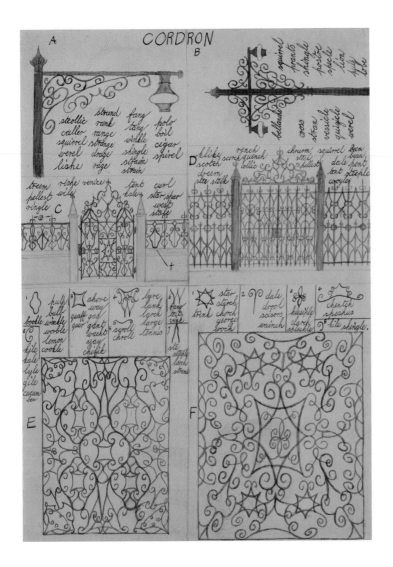

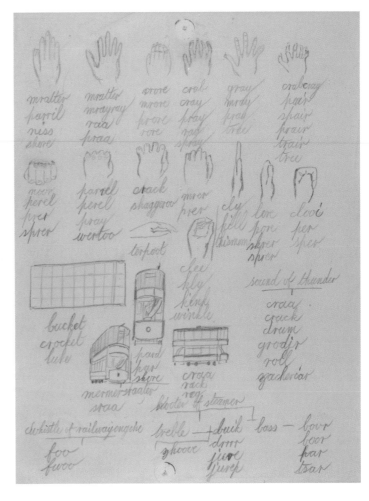

27. Gilbert Price
Cordron, undated
Ink and pencil on paper
36.9 × 25.9 cm
Bethlem Art and Collections Trust

28. Gilbert Price
Hand positions, undated
Pencil on paper
22.7 × 17.5 cm
Bethlem Art and Collections Trust

26. Adolf Wölfli
Fliehet vohr der Sünde, wie vohr einer Schlange, (recto/verso) c. 1928
Pencil and coloured pencil on paper
51 × 70.8 cm
Private collection

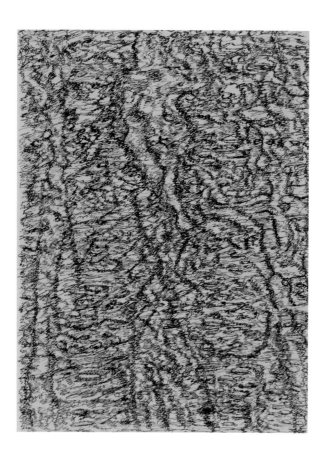

29. Henri Michaux
Untitled, 1959
Indian ink on paper
75 × 105 cm
Private collection, London

30. Mark Tobey
Blue Interior, 1959
Tempera on card
111.6 × 71 cm
Private collection, Switzerland

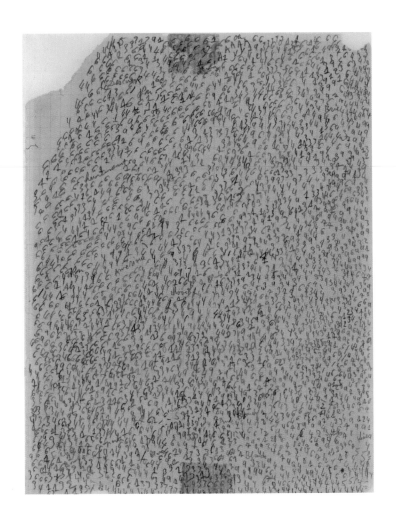

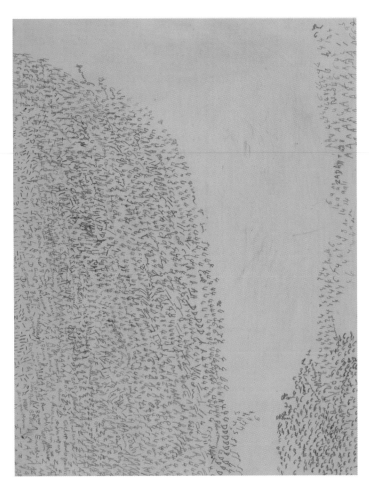

31. Anonymous
Doodle with numbers I, undated
Pencil on squared paper
22 × 16.8 cm
Bethlem Art and Collections Trust

32. Anonymous
Doodle with numbers II, 1955
Pencil on paper
20.9 × 26.8 cm
Bethlem Art and Collections Trust

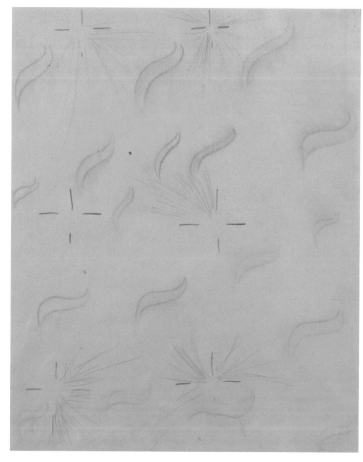

33. Anonymous
Frieze, undated
Graphite and coloured pencil on paper
30 × 23.9 cm
Bethlem Art and Collections Trust

34. Gillespie
Stars and Swirls, 15 March 1939
Coloured pencil crayons on paper
20.2 × 25.2 cm
Bethlem Art and Collections Trust

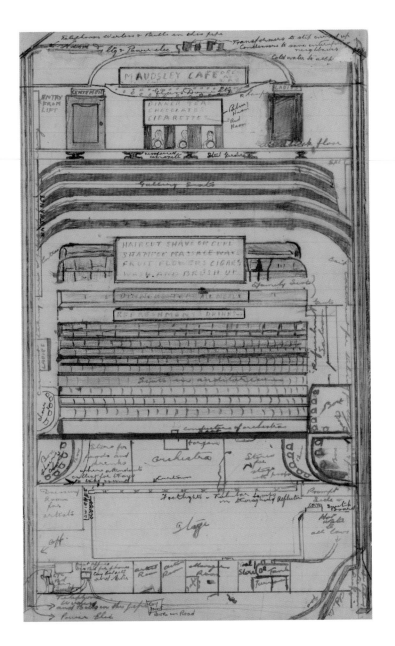

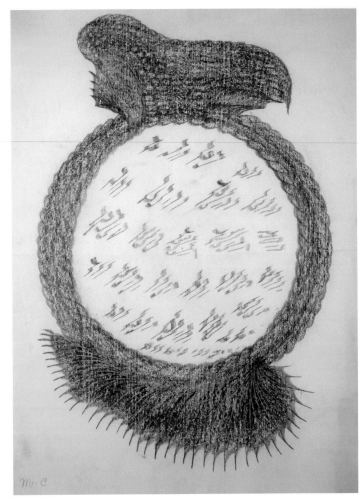

35. John Balnaves
Maudsley Café II, August 1936
Ink and coloured pencil on paper
32.6 × 19.8 cm
Bethlem Art and Collections Trust

36. Anonymous
Untitled, undated
Pencil and crayon on paper
38 × 27 cm
Collection Irish Museum of Modern Art
On loan from the Musgrave Kinley
Outsider Art Collection

Environments

Scattered throughout the world there are large environments, created by hand, such as painted temple compounds, mock castles, miniature cities and sculpture gardens populated with biblical and historical figures. Usually the culmination of years of obsessive work, these gardens or installations often express strong political or religious convictions. Colossal in scale, these environments bring together lifetimes of obsessive collecting, assembling and sculpting often using found materials to create a retreat or refuge.

They vary enormously from Emery Blagdon's *Healing Machines*, an extraordinary assemblage of wire structures densely hung in a rough farm shed in Nebraska to Charlie Yelton's bottle village in North Carolina, made of over 12,000 glass bottles. Based in Missouri, Jesse Howard covered his farm with hand painted signs often depicting truculent political messages painted in black letters on a white background. Paul Dobberstein created artificial grottoes encrusted with the rocks and precious stones he stockpiled for over a decade while Tom Every, a scrap artisan who owns a salvage and dismantling business has been building a huge sculpture park, since 1984, with pieces made from old cars and machine parts.

37. Jesse Howard
The Longest Word, c. 1975
Pencil and poster paint on wood
8 × 89 cm
Private collection

38. Jesse Howard
Free Thought. Free Speech c. 1978
Pencil and marker pen on linen
100 × 80.5 cm
Private collection

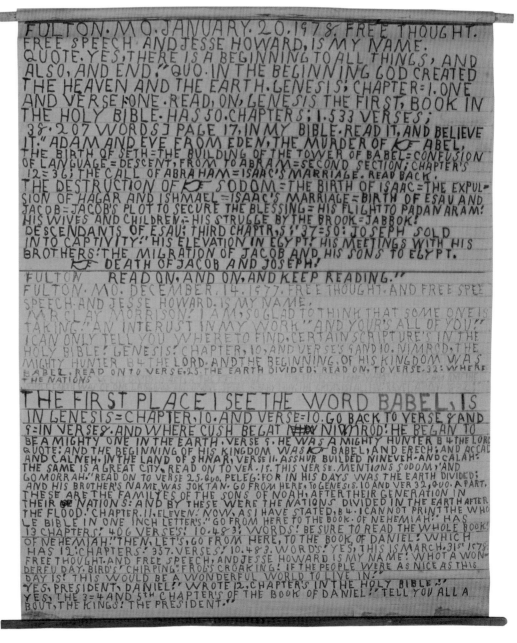

39. Emery Blagdon
Cascade #126, 257, 259 and *305*, c. 1956–1984
Steel wire, plastic, tin foil, wood, paper tape,
mixed media
190.5 × 17.8 × 10.2 cm
Private collection

40. Emery Blagdon
Untitled #491, 497, 499, c. 1956–1984
Wire, recycled aluminium cans
15.2 × 15.9 × 3.8 cm each
Private collection

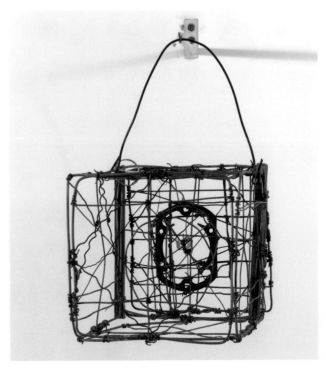

41. Emery Blagdon
Untitled #917, c. 1956–1984
Steel, copper wire, wood, tin foil,
mixed media
25.4 × 15.2 × 16.5 cm
Private collection

42. Emery Blagdon
Healing Machines, 1954–1986
North Platte, Nebraska

43. Charlie Yelton
Bottle Houses, 1971–1993
Forest City, North Carolina

44. Clyde Jones
Critter Crossing, since 1979
Bynum, North Carolina

45. W. C. Rice
The Cross Garden, 1976-2004
Prattville, Alabama

46. Tom Every
Forevertron, since 1983
Baraboo, Wisconsin

47. Father Paul M. Dobberstein
Grotto of the Redemption, 1912-1954
West Bend, Iowa

48. W. C. Rice
Prattville, Alabama

Madge Gill

Madge Gill's life and work was marked by traumatic personal tragedy. Born an illegitimate child in 1882, she was hidden away by her mother and aunt before being sent to an orphanage and subsequently to work as a servant in a farm in Canada. After returning to London she became a nurse in 1903 and lived with her aunt, who initiated her into spiritualism and astrology. At the age of twenty-five, she married and had three sons the second of whom died of influenza in 1918. The following year, Gill gave birth to a stillborn baby girl and was taken ill, spending several months in bed and losing the sight of her left eye. As a direct result of her attempts to contact her dead children, she began to paint and draw, usually working in bed by oil lamp but sometimes in complete darkness.

Although she denied being led by a spirit, she 'felt impelled to execute drawings' and was 'definitely guided by an unseen force'. This force, often called 'Myrninerest' in her drawings, was credited with inspiring her writings, embroideries and piano improvisations. She continuously depicted the female form – possibly representations of herself – in different moods, melancholic or fearful, haughty or almost triumphant. Dresses and hats are also abundantly represented and interwoven with architectural mazes and intense abstract lines, crosses and zigzags. Her white figures are engulfed by a mesmerising matrix of stairs, checkerboards and corridors that produce kaleidoscopic and vertiginous effects.

Gill was extremely prolific and, over forty years, produced thousands of drawings in all sizes, from postcards annotated with strange neologisms to large sheets of fabric, some of them over ten metres long. She often worked on paper or rolled calico, unrolling only a section at a time and never viewing the composition in its entirety. Gill rarely exhibited and was reluctant to sell her work during her lifetime, although she presented a number of drawings in the Whitechapel Gallery's East End Academy exhibitions in 1935, 1937, 1938 and 1947. By the time she died, in London's East End in 1961, she had hundreds of drawings piled under her bed and in her wardrobe.

49. Madge Gill
Untitled (Star), undated
Ink on paper
50 × 50 cm
London Borough of Newham
Heritage Services

50. Madge Gill
Untitled, undated
Ink on paper
62 × 50 cm
London Borough of Newham
Heritage Services

51. Madge Gill
Untitled, c. 1950
Pen and ink on card
63 × 50 cm
Private collection

52. Madge Gill
Untitled (landscape), undated
Ink on paper
61.9 × 50 cm
London Borough of Newham
Heritage Services

Faces and Masks

From the middle of the 19th century modern painting and sculpture saw a return to the use of the human face as mask. Where portraiture had dominated since the Renaissance, artists began to see the face as a primitive, emblematic site, replete with transformative and magical powers. Edmund Monsiel, for example, is known for the chaotic and hallucinogenic agglomerations of figures, faces and eyes, often referring to religious themes, which cover every corner of his paper. Scottie Wilson's favourite subjects were usually melancholic self-portraits with big noses often accompanied by strange marine creatures or tortoise-like figures with bulbous and exaggerated eyes. Within his works he created a personal moral code with characters called 'evils' and 'greedies'

juxtaposed with naturalistic symbols of goodness and truth. Produced as his mental state approached a crisis, the legendary dancer Nijinsky claimed that the drawing presented here, one of a series of stylised portraits based on circular motions, represented a soldier's face. After producing a series of watercolours in the late 1940s in which he claimed faces would appear out of the paper of their own accord, Henri Michaux protested that he lived an 'excessively facial existence'. Jean-Michel Basquiat first became famous by spray-painting graffiti on subway cars and slum buildings in New York but, in the early 1980s, he used painterly gestures on canvas, often depicting skeletal figures and mask-like faces that expressed his obsession with mortality.

54. Michel Nedjar
Paris Belleville, 1985
Technical pencil on paper
49.5 × 64.5 cm
Collection Irish Museum of Modern Art
Private collection

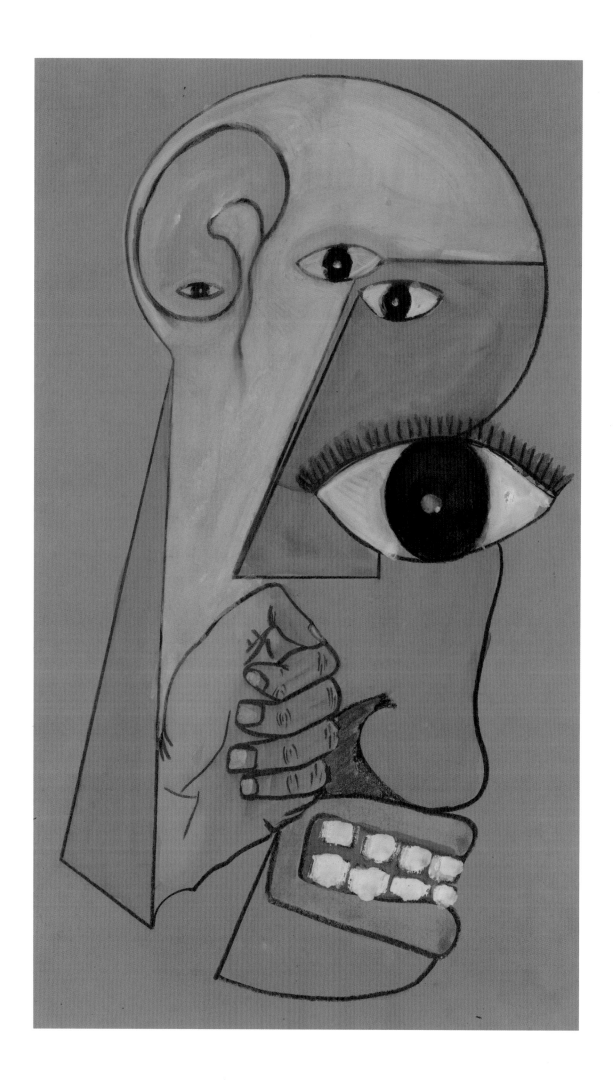

54

56. Theo (Theodor Wagemann)
Hitler der Führer Attolf Hitler, undated
Crayon and pencil on paper
37.4 × 25.5 cm
Collection Irish Museum of Modern Art
On loan from the Musgrave Kinley
Outsider Art Collection

57. Theo (Theodor Wagemann)
The King of Prussia R.I.P., undated
Crayon and pencil on paper
37.4 × 25.5 cm
Collection Irish Museum of Modern Art
On loan from the Musgrave Kinley
Outsider Art Collection

55. Patrick Joseph McDonagh
Body, c. 1966–1977
Charcoal and gouache on paper
44.4 × 26.4 cm
Bethlem Art and Collections Trust

58. Scottie Wilson
Untitled (with Swans, Clowns
and Greedies), c.1940–1945
Ink and watercolour on paper
36.6 × 25.4 cm
Bethlem Art and Collections Trust

59. Vaslav Nijinsky
A Mask, c.1919
Coloured pencil on paper
37.7 × 28.3 cm
Bethlem Art and Collections Trust

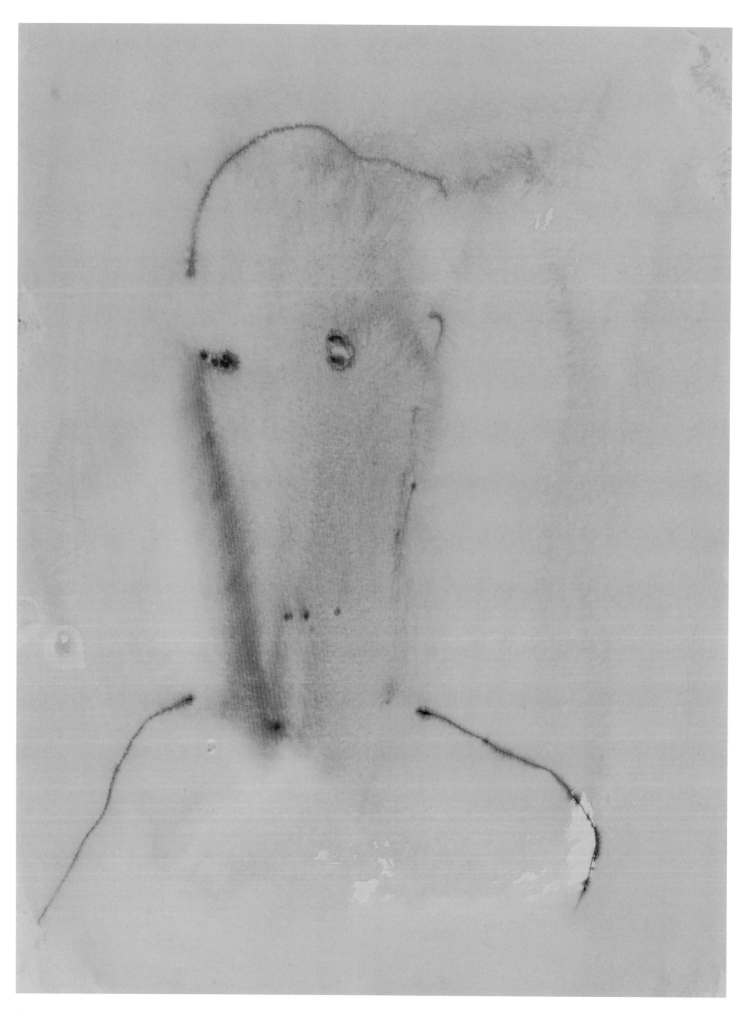

60. Henri Michaux
Untitled, 1946–48
Watercolour on paper
31 × 23 cm
Private collection, London

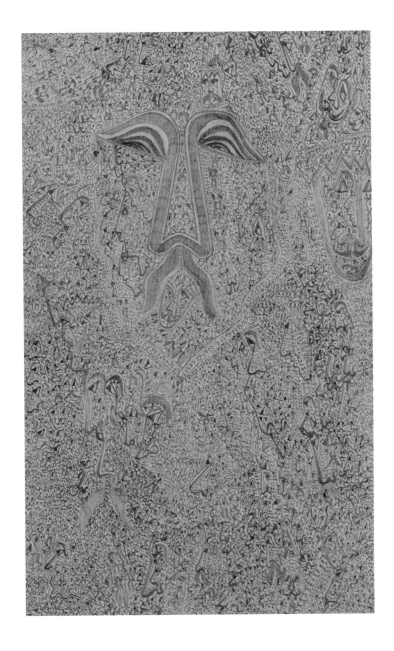

61. Edmund Monsiel
Untitled, c. 1943
Pencil on card
17.5 × 11.5 cm
Private collection

62. Edmund Monsiel
Untitled, c. 1956
Pencil on card
15.5 × 9.5 cm
Private collection

The Erotic Body

The image of the body has been used as a site for erotic projection by artists since the time of the cave dwellers. It was given particular prominence in the evolution of modern art by such influential figures as Paul Gauguin, Ludwig Kirchner and Pablo Picasso through their fascination with the art of 'primitive' cultures. This section includes diverse representations of the body, ranging from explicit and erotically charged depictions to raw, primal effigies and rhythmic or libidinous dances.

The most explicit example is by the Austrian expressionist Alfred Kubin, an artist of dark, troubling forces—the satanic, the erotic and the endless cycle of death and pleasure. His ink drawing, *Kuss* (Kiss), was probably a reaction to the sudden death of his fiancé.

Although not explicitly sexual, Louis Soutter's compositions are often dominated by human figures engaged in strange rituals and bacchanalian dances. From 1937, he painted with his fingers often using the theme of the crucifixion as a metaphor for his vision of suffering and alienation. Eduardo Paolozzi was inspired by artists like Alberto Giacometti and Jean Dubuffet to create the raw, primal sculpture *Robot,* 1956, which was modelled from a miscellany of machine parts. Von Stropp's *Oestrum* is a large, dense and intricate depiction of anatomical parts surrounded by an assortment of eggs, leaves, phallic shapes, lion-like creatures and faces. The word *oestrum* refers to a state of heightened sexual arousal and activity in non-human mammals.

63. Eduardo Paolozzi
Robot, 1956
Bronze with gold brown patina
48.3 × 21 × 14.2 cm
Private collection, London

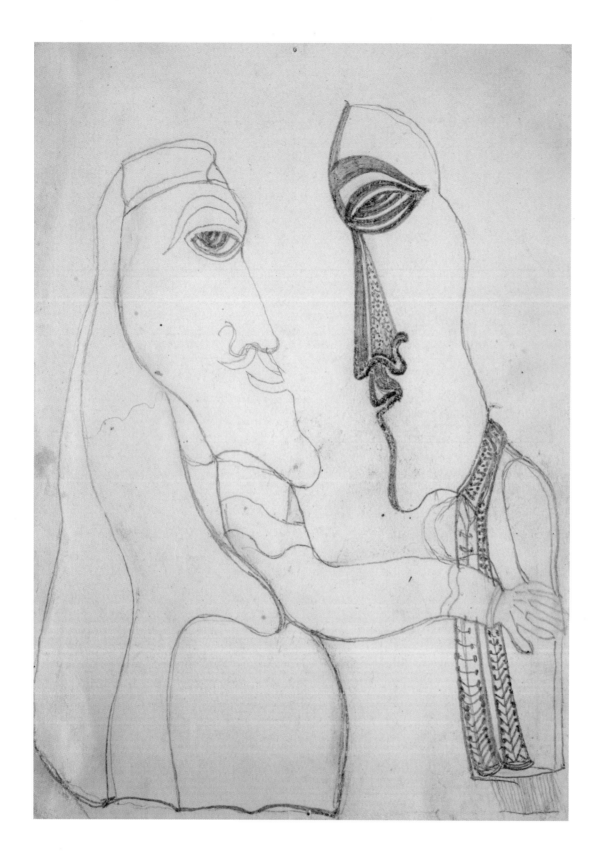

64. Edmund Monsiel
Untitled, undated
Pencil on paper
15.5 × 10.5 cm
Collection Irish Museum of Modern Art
On loan from the Musgrave Kinley
Outsider Art Collection

65. Louis Soutter
Two Personations, 1937–42
Finger print drawing
44 × 57 cm
Private collection, London

66. Alfred Kubin
Kuss (Kiss), 1903
Ink on paper
31.6 × 39.5 cm
Private collection, courtesy
Richard Nagy, London

67. Von Stropp
Oestrum, 1985
Acrylic, polyfilla and board
183.5 × 122 cm
Bethlem Art and Collections Trust

68. Von Stropp
The Five, c. 1985–1990
Pencil on paper
54.8 × 37.1 cm
Bethlem Art and Collections Trust

Fantastic Dreams
and Haunting Tales

Storytelling has held a fascination for painters of every period. At its most ambitious it takes the form of 'history painting', modern examples of which include Pablo Picasso's *Guernica*, 1937, Renato Guttuso's *Flight from Etna,* 1940 and Larry Rivers' *Washington Crossing the Delaware,* 1953. Many artists are compelled to address the strangeness of their lives and reflect on the shapes and textures that surround them. On one hand, they might channel an undeviating honesty and urgency into their work, constructing authentic meaning through a highly charged dialogue with materials. More modestly it surfaces as the depiction of local events, domestic and personal tales as well as semi-private fantasies.

The Reverend William A. Blayney used painting to warn about the decline of morals in the world. He is represented here by a colourful, but intense and apocalyptic, scene. William Kurelek's *The Nightmare* represents a figure, possibly the artist, huddled up on a bed surrounded by grotesque animals and violent and aggressive scenes. The artist, teacher and writer Julian Trevelyan became associated with Surrealism and produced the drawing *Stage II* after being administred with mescaline in a medical experiment at London's Maudsley Hospital. There are three delicate drawings from the Bethlem Royal Hospital by an anonymous artist that depict the actions of a woman being restrained in what appears to be a hospital room. Although impossible to tell, these drawings may represent harrowing personal experiences or paranoid delusions.

69. Rev. William A Blayney
*Dispensationals Periods of the Dragon
Devil Satan*, early 1960s
Oil and poster paint on board
62.2 × 70 cm
Private collection

70. William Kurelek
The Nightmare, c. 1953
Pencil on paper
75 × 55 cm
Bethlem Art and Collections Trust

71. Margery Penfold
Despair I, 14 April 1936
Watercolour on paper
28 × 18.7 cm
Bethlem Art and Collections Trust

72. Edgar Farrar
Head and Music in Surrealist Landscape, 1943
Pencil or black ink and varnish on paper
stuck onto wood
21.5 × 14.2 cm
Bethlem Art and Collections Trust

Stage II.   J. O. Trustgen

73. Julian Trevelyan
Stage II, 1936
Pencil on paper
19.1 × 17.7 cm
Bethlem Art and Collections Trust

74. Anonymous
Bound Woman in Cellar, 29 January 1937
Pencil on paper
25 × 20 cm
Bethlem Art and Collections Trust

75. Anonymous
Girl Tied to Post, 29 January 1937
Pencil on paper
22.7 × 17.4 cm
Bethlem Art and Collections Trust

76. Anonymous
Kneeling Bound Girl, 29 January 1937
Pencil on paper
18.5 × 16.5 cm
Bethlem Art and Collections Trust

Biographies

Pearl Alcock
Born in 1934 in Jamaica but lives and works in London. Alcock paints Jamaican landscapes and what she terms 'mood' pictures, many of which are in the Musgrave Kinley *Outsider* Art Collection. These pictures deal with imagery from dreams and draw heavily on Jamaican spirituality.

Angelus
The Swiss artist Angelus (1910–1993) was only 'discovered' at the age of 76 although he had already been making art for many years. His works are informed by deep philosophical enquiry and concerns about religion, globalisation and the environment.

Jean-Michel Basquiat [Cat. 4]
Born in 1960, Jean-Michel Basquiat first became known as a graffiti artist in New York City using the infamous signature of SAMO, meaning 'Same Old Shit', before shooting to fame and fortune on the international art scene of the 1980s. He used painterly gestures on canvas to depict imagery from urban life including automobiles, buildings and the police. Many of the writings and collages in his work relate to his black and Puerto Rican identity. He collaborated with pop artist Andy Warhol from 1983 and died of a heroin overdose in 1988.

Emery Blagdon [Cat. 39–42]
Emery Blagdon (1907–1986) was a farmer who lived on the southern edge of the Sandhills of north-central Nebraska. From 1954-1986, he created *Healing Machines* that he believed generated an electromagnetic energy that could alleviate pain and prevent or cure disease. Assembled structures made from copper wire, aluminium, foil, ribbon, beads, magnets and a variety of found items, the *Healing Machines* were installed in a farm shed.

Reverend William A. Blayney [Cat. 69]
Born in Western Pennsylvania in 1918, William A. Blayney painted cartoon-like figures and texts on bomber planes while serving during World War II. After intense bible study he discovered a vocation for preaching. In 1957 Blayney began to express his concern with the decline of morality through painting. His paintings mostly depict the book of Revelations and the redemptive power of God as revealed by the Hebrew prophet Daniel. He was ordained in 1969 in the Pentecostal Ministry by the laying on of hands and died in 1985.

Francois Burland
Francois Burland was born in Lausanne, Switzerland in 1958 and now lives on a farm in Chexbres, Switzerland. His work evolved out of an interest in Greek and Celtic mythology as well as the Dogon cosmology and the indigenous culture of American Indians and Australian Aborigines. Also inspired by the magic and rituals of the nomadic tribes that he discovered on his travels, notably to the Sahara desert, his favoured medium is ballpoint pen on Kraft paper.

Eugene von Bruenchenhein [Cat. 12]
Born in Wisconsin, Eugene von Bruenchenhein (1910–1983) was a baker who was fascinated with botany and science. He devised extensive metaphysical theories about a genetically encoded collective knowledge and composed reams of poetry on nature, love, war and imaginary travels through time and space. Driven by 'unknown forces', he produced intricate, brightly coloured finger paintings of atomic mushrooms, radiating hearts, mythical sea creatures, fantastical landscapes and futuristic metropolises.

James Castle [Cat. 25]
Born in Idaho, James Castle (1900–1977) was profoundly deaf and is believed never to have learned to read and write. His works are generally small in scale and produced exclusively from found materials such as packaging, mail and food containers. Castle painstakingly inked real and altered alphabets and produced numerous books with pages of numbers, symbols, facsimile postcards, comic strip images and advertisements taken from periodicals and catalogues.

Henry Darger [Cat. 17–21, Cat. 77]
Born in 1892, Henry Darger's place of birth is still debated. He was honourably discharged from the US Army, for physical and psychological reasons, only a few months after being drafted in 1917. He was a reclusive writer and illustrator who worked as a caretaker in a Chicago hospital. It was only after his death that a 15,000-page fantasy manuscript called The *Story of the Vivian Girls* was discovered, along with several thousand watercolours and drawings. He died in 1973 in a Catholic mission operated by the Little Sisters of the Poor.

Serge Delaunay
Serge Delaunay was born in 1956 in Charleroi, Belgium. Driven by a passion for automobiles and engineering, he creates precise drawings of machinery, car parts, robots, cosmonauts

and various architectural forms. He also produces drawings of space bases and cosmic machines in other universes and galaxies, often surrounded by planets and stars. These technical or scientific depictions of a futurist and extra-terrestrial world are usually made with a black marker pen and accompanied by texts that comment on the machines' exploits.

Charles Dellschau [Cat. 13–16]

Born in 1830, Charles Dellschau emigrated from Prussia to Texas in the 1850s. Although little is known about his life, twelve scrapbooks were discovered in 1967, forty years after his death. From their coded writings and images, it seems that Dellschau had belonged to a secret society called the Sonora Aero Club consisting of sixty-two members committed to designing and assembling aircraft. The watercolour images of flying machines are heavily ornamented and are accompanied by newspaper cuttings heralding trans-Atlantic flights, early passenger dirigibles and notices about heroic mechanical innovations.

Father Paul M. Dobberstein [Cat. 47]

Paul Matthias Dobberstein was born in Rosenfeld, Germany in 1872 and emigrated to America in 1892. He entered the Seminary of St. Francis near Milwaukee to prepare for the Priesthood and was appointed pastor of Saint Peter and Paul's Catholic Church in West Bend in 1904. He started building the Grotto of the Redemption in 1912 and continued building it until his death in 1954.

Janko Domsic [Cat. 1]

The Croatian artist Janko Domsic (1915–1983) is believed to have immigrated to France in the 1930s where he worked on the railway. His coloured pencil and ballpoint drawings and their texts present a combination of biography and a kind of mathematical philosophy of the world. His figures represent some kind of 'microcosmic man' and his language, images and symbols, often drawn in circular movements, refer to mystic ideas, the moral code of freemasons and economics.

Jean Dubuffet [Cat. 6]

Born in 1901, in Le Havre, France, Jean Dubuffet attended art classes in his youth and moved to Paris in 1918 to study at the Académie Julian although he left after only six months. During this time, he became fascinated with Hans Prinzhorn's book on 'psychopathic' art. From 1945, he collected *Art Brut*, spontaneously produced works by untutored individuals,

including patients with mental illnesses, now permanently housed in Lausanne. One of the major French artists of the last century, Dubuffet was very influenced by the art he collected and died in Paris in 1985.

Tom Every [Cat. 46]

Tom Every (also known as Dr. Evermor) was born in Wisconsin in 1938, Remembering the patriotic collecting and recycling of newspapers, rags, and toothpaste tubes during the war, Every formed his own company, the Wisconsin By-Products Corporation and has been building a huge sculpture park environment using scrap material since 1984, The combined pieces made from old cars and machine parts are known as the 'Forevertron Set'.

Willem van Genk [Cat. 10]

Willem van Genk was born in 1927 in The Netherlands. The only boy in a family of eight he was placed in an orphanage when his mother died. His drawings explore the distant places he would personally like to visit. He draws and makes collages with the underlying belief that 'the world is one vast plot'.

Madge Gill [Cat. 3, Cat. 49–53]

Madge Gill was born in London in 1884. She grew up in an orphanage and in the care of an elderly aunt. Gill was interested in spiritualism and believed that her intricate drawings and embroideries were the work of a spirit she called 'Myrninerest'. Her large-scale drawings on paper and calico (some are more than 10m long) had to be worked on a roll, so only part of the work was visible as she worked.

Annie Hooper

Annie Hooper, lived on a remote island off the coast of North Carolina. A deeply religious housewife and Sunday-school teacher, halfway through her long life Hooper began to discern the shapes of animals or people in ordinary objects. She used these shapes to create sculptures illustrating scenes from the Bible and spent the remaining 35 years of her life filling her white-frame house, with thousands of biblical figures made of wood and concrete. She died in 1986.

Jesse Howard [Cat. 37–38]

Born in 1885, Jesse Howard was a farmer who took to reading the Bible and making sign paintings after he retired in Missouri. Howard's opinions on wide-ranging subjects like politics, religion, freedom of speech, his local town and the state of the world were scattered on panels throughout his farm. He also used pieces of coloured glass, marbles, metal, leather (soles of shoes) and window blinds for his comments which were written in distinctive black letters with occasional words in gold, green or red lettering on a white background. He died in 1983.

Clyde Jones [Cat. 44]
Clyde Jones was born in North Carolina in either 1938 or 1939. He attended school intermittently and worked as a day labourer, construction worker and pulpwood logger. In 1979, while recovering from a leg injury, he started to make carvings inspired by shapes in his woodpile. He creates rough hewn figures or animals by using a chainsaw or nailing roots and stumps together. Jones incorporates found objects such as bottle tops, film containers, plastic flowers and fruit in the sculptures and began painting with enamel and oil-based paint in 1987.

Wassily Kandinsky [Cat. 7]
Wassily Kandinsky was born in Moscow in 1866 and studied law and economics before moving to Germany to study art in 1897. He co-founded the ground-breaking *Der Blaue Reiter* (The Blue Rider) group and began to conceive of painting as a pathway to spirituality. He increasingly reduced recognisable elements, like landscapes and horse riders, to calligraphic lines. At the same time, he painted large areas of vibrant colour to stimulate emotions associated with music. He died near Paris in 1944.

Alfred Kubin [Cat. 66]
Alfred Kubin was born in Bohemia in 1877. Having begun as an apprentice in photography, he enrolled in the Academy of Fine Arts in Munich. In 1911, he joined the newly founded *Der Blaue Reiter* and exhibited with his friends Paul Klee and Franz Marc. Influenced by James Ensor, Francisco de Goya and Odilon Redon, he created thousands of pen-and-ink drawings, portfolios – including the famous *Totentanz* (Dance of the Dead), 1925 – and illustrations for more than 70 books by authors like Fyodor Dostoevsky, E.T.A. Hoffmann, Edgar Allan Poe, Gérard de Nerval and August Strindberg. He died in Austria in 1959.

William Kurelek [Cat. 70]
William Kurelek (1927–1977) was raised on rural farms in Alberta and Manitoba. Around 1946 his first symptoms of schizophrenia began to appear and, in 1952, he travelled to London seeking medical treatment. For the next year and a half he was a resident,

and then an out-patient, of Maudsley Psychiatric Hopital. His most famous work, *The Maze*, 1953, is an autobiographical self-portait, which depicts scenes of persecution and delusion compartmentalised in his split-open head. Shortly after leaving London, Kurelek found religion and began painting landscapes of Canada and religious works.

Augustin Lesage [Cat. 5, Cat. 9]
Augustin Lesage (1876–1954) was a miner in the Pas-de-Calais who heard voices ordering him to paint when he was thirty-five years old. He painted hundreds of works charged with religious symbols, inspired by Buddhist, Egyptian, Christian, Hindu, Indo-Chinese, Tibetan or Persian culture. The Surrealists were interested in Lesage's symmetrical, repetitive style and his use of small decorative elements that include architectural and anthropomorphic figures.

Raphael Lonné
Lonné, born in 1910 in Monfort en Chalosse, France, came from a family of farm labourers. He showed an early interest in literature and music and became interested in spiritualism in the 1940s. Having began to draw under the influence of spirits, his drawing career ended as suddenly as it began when he felt that his spirit-guide had departed. He resumed drawing in the 1960s when he felt reconnected with the spirits. He died in 1989.

Albert Louden
Albert Louden was born in 1943. He was a London truck driver but contacted Victor Musgrave after the *Outsiders* exhibition at the Hayward Gallery, London in 1979. The figures he paints in broad, flat colours have a Surreal and generally discomforting relationship to their environment.

Dwight Mackintosh
Born in 1906, the Californian Mackintosh was institutionalised when he was sixteen years old. On his release fifty-six years later, he began to attend art classes in the Creative Growth Art Centre in Oakland. Over the following twenty years he produced numerous drawing of figures, buildings and vehicles combined with illegible written texts. He died in 1999.

Roberto Matta [Cat. 8]
Roberto Sebastian Antonio Matta Echaurren was born in Santiago, Chile in 1911. He studied architecture before travelling to Paris in 1933 where he worked in the architect

Le Corbusier's studio. On a visit to Madrid, he met the poet and dramatist Federico García Lorca and the poet Pablo Neruda who introduced him to the artists Salvador Dalí and André Breton. Impressed by Matta's drawings, Breton invited him to join the Surrealist group in 1937 when he began to explore the subconscious and to develop an imagery of cosmic creation and destruction. He died in 2002 in Italy.

Henri Michaux [Cat. 29, Cat. 60]
Henri Michaux was born in the Belgian town of Namur in 1899. Having initially wanted to become a priest, he abandoned medical studies to sign on as a seaman. After reading works by Lautréamont, he began to write in 1922 and subsequently produced over thirty internationally acclaimed books. In 1925, he met Paul Klee, Max Ernst and Giorgio de Chirico and began to paint and draw in an attempt to escape from the 'conventions of language'. In the mid 1950s he experimented with hallucinatory drugs, particularly mescaline. He died in Paris in 1984.

Edmund Monsiel [Cat. 61–62, 64]
Edmund Monsiel was born in Poland in 1897 and died in 1967. After hiding in his brother's attic for the duration of World War II, he experienced delusions and possibly hallucinations. In the last twenty years of his life, he produced a body of exquisitely detailed drawings on small scraps of paper, of which only 500 exist. His artistic outpourings were often filled with religious inscriptions and visual hallucinations of Christ and the Devil, before giving way to chaotic agglomerations of figures and faces. The strongest features in the drawings are faces with moustaches, often set within a background of hundreds of pairs of staring eyes.

J. B. Murry
Murry was born in 1910 in the USA and died in 1989. His work was brought to Monika Kinley's attention by his doctor, William Rawlings, in the 1980s. A farmer all his life, Murry turned to drawing and 'spirit writing' in old age, producing pages of illegible 'writing'.

Michel Nedjar [Cat. 54]
Nedjar was born in 1947 in France. He lives and works in Paris but has travelled to India, Mexico and North Africa, in pursuit of his interest in 'primitive' religions. He makes dolls, which have voodoo and totemic qualities as well as three dimensional objects and reliefs in papier maché. With Madeleine Lommell he is co-founder of L'Aracine, a Museum for Art Brut, in France. Recently Nedjar has also begun to make films.

Vaslav Fomich Nijinsky [Cat. 59]
Vaslav Fomich Nijinsky (1890–1950) was a legendary Polish-born Russian ballet dancer and choreographer. The Russian impresario Sergei Diaghilev, became Nijinsky's mentor and lover and was heavily involved in developing his outstanding career. In 1916 during a North American tour, signs of dementia praecox became apparent to members of the dance company. Nijinsky had a nervous breakdown in 1919 and was diagnosed with schizophrenia. He spent the rest of his life in and out of psychiatric hospitals and asylums and died in a London clinic.

Eduardo Paolozzi [Cat. 63]
Born in Edinburgh, Scotland in 1924, Paolozzi studied at the Ruskin School of Art and the Slade School of Art in London. He subsequently moved to Paris and was influenced by Dada and Surrealism. On his return to London in 1949, he shared a studio with Lucian Freud and came into contact with Francis Bacon. In 1951, while working as professor at the Central School of Art & Design, London, he won his first important sculptural commission. His work as a printmaker, ceramicist and above all, sculptor, is of major importance. He died in 2005.

Perifimou (Alexander Georgiou)
Alexander Georgiou, better known as Perifimou was born in 1916 in Cyprus. He came to London as a young adult and worked there until his death in 2001. Victor Musgrave discovered Perifimou when he was working as an attendant at the Tate Gallery. He made drawings that refer to Cypriot myths and beliefs, working from small postcard sized templates to larger paintings.

Valerie Potter
Potter was born in 1954 in Tenterden, Kent and travelled widely with her parents before being diagnosed with schizophrenia in her late teens. She briefly attended Hull College of Art but left after one term, having been described as having 'no talent'. She paints, draws and embroiders, combining a classical approach to composition with a sense of the tragic and the absurd.

W. C. Rice [Cat. 45, Cat. 48]
W. C. Rice, a visionary folk figure, was born in 1930 in Alabama. Rice claimed not to be an artist but a born again man, on a mission to save souls and warn others of the dangers of sinful living. His

Miracle Cross Garden was filled with rough wooden crosses and hand lettered signs with religious sayings, red paint symbolising the blood of Jesus and biblical admonitions. He began erecting his first crosses in 1976 after receiving instructions from God to erect three wooden crosses as a permanent tribute to his recently deceased mother. He died in 2004.

Vollis Simpson

Vollis Simpson was born in 1919. After retiring from his machinery repair business in 1985, he devoted his free time to creating wind-powered artworks. The High Museum of Art in Atlanta accepted Simpson's fanciful and functional windmills into their collection in 1987. A decade later, whirligigs were sought for the 1996 Olympics in Atlanta. Simpson made four sculptures: a man sawing, a man on a unicycle, a man pumping water and a duck, all of which were installed throughout the city centre.

Louis Soutter [Cat. 65]

Born in Morges, Switzerland in 1871, Soutter studied engineering, architecture, music and painting and for a time taught in an art school in the USA. Mentally disturbed when he returned to Switzerland in 1906, he spent a year in a private clinic. He worked as a professional musician until 1923 when he was hospitalised again in a clinic in the Jura where he remained until his death in 1942.

Von Stropp [Cat. 67–68]

Born in Stanwell, England, in 1962, Von Stropp is known to have used over a hundred pseudonyms. During a childhood, that he has described as 'grey, overcast, an eternal hangover', he taught himself to draw and paint. Aged eleven, he began to have ecstatic, visionary experiences and started to paint obsessively shortly after leaving school. Von Stropp's work displays extreme attention to detail in many entangled still lifes that often feature eggs, rabbits, birds and dense foliage.

Theo (Theodor Wagemann) [Cat. 56–57]

'Theo' was born in 1918 in Germany. A traumatic experience in his early teens changed him from a sociable child into a silent reclusive one. Under the Nazi regime he was forcefully sterilized but escaped euthanasia due to the intervention of a doctor and returned to his family. Following hospitalisation in 1977, he began to draw obsessively taking his subjects from the bible and from history. He died in 1998.

Mark Tobey [Cat. 30]

Mark Tobey was born in 1890, in Wisconsin. In 1918 he converted to the Bahà'i World Faith, which led him to explore the representation of the spiritual in art. He also began to explore Chinese calligraphy and went to Paris in 1925, beginning his lifelong travels. While in the Middle East, he became interested in Persian and Arabic script. After several journeys to Mexico and the Orient, Tobey spent a month in a Zen monastery outside Kyoto in 1934; the following year he began his 'white writing' paintings. In 1958, Tobey was awarded the painting prize at the Venice *Biennale*. He settled in Basel in 1960, where he lived until his death in 1976.

Bill Traylor [Cat. 11]

Traylor was born a slave on the George Hartwell Traylor plantation near Benton, Alabama, in 1856. He was self-taught and began drawing in 1939, producing approximately 1800 drawings over a period of about three years. He used a straight edge to create geometric silhouettes of human and animal figures which he then filled in with crayon and tempera. He is known for his intriguing use of pattern versus flat colour and an intuitive sense of space. He started hanging his works on street fence to entertain the locals. He died in Montgomery in 1949.

Julian Trevelyan [Cat. 73]

Julian Trevelyan was a painter, printmaker, teacher and writer, born in Surrey in 1910 and educated at Cambridge University, where he became acquainted with Surrealism. For several years in the early 1930s, he studied alongside such figures as Max Ernst, Oskar Kokoschka, Joan Miró and Pablo Picasso in Paris and joined the English Surrealist Group in 1936. Using a variety of styles, his pictures retain a dreamlike, often childlike, fantastical quality. At London's Maudsley Hospital, Trevelyan was one of a number of painters who was selected as a guinea-pig for medical research into the effects of mescaline: 'I have been given the Key of the Universe', he wrote in his memoirs. He died in 1988.

Oswald Tschirtner

Tschirtner was born in 1920 in Austria. He wanted to become a priest but following conscription into the Austrian army and experiences in World War II he became ill and was institutionalised. He lives in the Artist's House in Gugging where he produces small or very large images of human figures.

Shafique Uddin

Uddin was born in Bangladesh in 1962 but moved to East London where he now lives and works. He has painted since childhood, using his art to communicate events and rituals from Bangladeshi culture and the experience of living in London. His output is prolific and his work has been exhibited in London (including the Whitechapel Open in 1983) and New York.

Pascal Verbena

Verbena was born in Marseilles in 1941. After variously working as a sailor, a fisherman and a post office official he decided, in 1995, to devote himself to making art. He writes poetry and makes objects from wood that is specially selected from river mouths and quiet beaches. He makes elaborate 'habitacles' places in which to hide precious found objects from nature or old photographs and memorabilia, which have a personal significance.

Scottie Wilson [Cat. 58]

Scottie Wilson was born in London in 1888 but grew up in Scotland. He served in the First World War and then moved to Canada. While running a second hand shop in Toronto he began doodling with a fountain pen. His work was collected by Picasso and Dubuffet and he became well-known as an exhibitor in London where he returned in 1945. Wilson's drawings reveal an infatuation with nature as well as his battle with darker forces in life that he termed 'the Greedys'. He died in 1972.

Agatha Wojciechowsky

Almost nothing is known about Agatha Wojciechowsky's life. She was born in Steinach, Germany in 1896 and claimed to have been in contact with spirits from the age of four. In 1923 she emigrated to America where she worked as a cleaner, seamstress and kitchen hand before becoming known as a medium with powers of healing. She started to produce automatic drawings in 1951 and was collected by artist Marcel Duchamp.

Adolf Wölfi [Cat. 2, Cat. 26]

Adolf Wölfli was born in 1864 near Berne, Switzerland. He worked as a farm hand but was accused of child molestation and was committed to the asylum in Berne in 1895 where he remained until his death in 1930. He was subject to violent outbursts and was kept isolated in a one-man cell, which he filled with manuscripts and drawings. Much of his work relates to his self-canonisation as the fictitious 'St Adolf II'.

Charlie Yelton [Cat. 43]

In 1971, Charlie Yelton began building his bottle houses in Forest City, North Carolina. After his retirement, he saw a bottle house on television and spent the next four years and nearly 12,000 bottles building three bottle houses, a glass wishing well and a glass flower planter out of beer, whiskey, 7-Up and Milk of Magnesia bottles. He died in 1993 at the age of 84.

Anna Zemankova

The Czech artist, Anna Zemankova was born in 1908. Dissuaded from a career as an artist by her father she began to make art in middle age. Her extraordinary botanical imagery was created using a combination of drawing, cutting-out and stitching. She believed that she was merely the vehicle for a spiritual force that guided her. For greater privacy and concentration she worked at night. She died in 1986.

Note: Information about many of the artists in this publication is often difficult to obtain, vague and conflicting. The information is provided only as a simple introduction and will hopefully prompt further research. The artists not listed here are absent through lack of information at the current time.

List of Works not reproduced

Pearl Alcock
Dance of the bones, 1987
31 × 35 cm
Collection Irish Museum of Modern Art.
Private collection

Angelus
*Die Triebwelt [Driving Force
of the World],* undated
Pencil, crayon and ballpoint pen
29.5 × 21 cm
Collection Irish Museum of Modern Art,
on loan from the Musgrave Kinley
Outsider Art Collection, Dublin

Anonymous
Botanical garden, undated
Coloured pencil on paper
11.7 × 18.1 cm
Bethlem Art and Collections Trust

Anonymous
Untitled, undated
Pencil on paper
21 × 17 cm
Collection Irish Museum of Modern Art,
on loan from the Musgrave Kinley
Outsider Art Collection, Dublin

Anonymous
Untitled, undated
Pencil on paper
28 × 20.5 cm
Collection Irish Museum of Modern Art,
on loan from the Musgrave Kinley
Outsider Art Collection, Dublin

Anonymous
Untitled, undated
Pencil & crayon on paper
38 × 27 cm
Collection Irish Museum of Modern Art,
on loan from the Musgrave Kinley
Outsider Art Collection, Dublin

John Balnaves
Maudsley café I, August 1936
Graphite and coloured pencil on paper
33.5 × 22.9 cm
Bethlem Art and Collections Trust

Baron, E.
Deformed monkey with clouds, 1941–49?
Graphite on paper
19 × 13.8 cm
Bethlem Art and Collections Trust

Francois Burland
Untitled, undated
Crayon on paper
70 × 212 cm
Collection Irish Museum of Modern Art,
on loan from the Musgrave Kinley
Outsider Art Collection, Dublin

Henry Darger
Side A. At Journal, undated
Watercolour and pencil on assembled paper
48 × 178 cm
Collection Irish Museum of Modern Art,
on loan from the Musgrave Kinley
Outsider Art Collection, Dublin

Serge Delaunay
Untitled, undated
Felt tip pen on paper
83 × 64 cm
Collection Irish Museum of Modern Art,
on loan from the Musgrave Kinley
Outsider Art Collection, Dublin

Patrick Joseph McDonagh
Eyed body, 1966–1977?
Charcoal and gouache on paper
41.5 × 32.5 cm
Bethlem Art and Collections Trust

Raphael Lonné
Untitled, 1977
Ink on paper
40 × 54.5 cm
Collection Irish Museum of Modern Art,
on loan from the Musgrave Kinley
Outsider Art Collection, Dublin

Francis Marshall
Sans Famille, 1977
Wood, string, stuffed materials
52.5 × 40.3 × 12 cm
Collection Irish Museum of Modern Art,
on loan from the Musgrave Kinley
Outsider Art Collection, Dublin

Sean Molloy
Untitled, 1989
Ink on paper
59 × 41 cm
Collection Irish Museum of Modern Art,
on loan from the Musgrave Kinley
Outsider Art Collection, Dublin

William M.G. Murray
War, 1943
Graphite, ink and watercolour on paper
20.3 × 25.3 cm
Bethlem Art and Collections Trust

J. B. Murry
Untitled, undated
Paint & felt tip pen on card
71 × 56 cm
Collection Irish Museum of Modern Art,
on loan from the Musgrave Kinley
Outsider Art Collection, Dublin

Michel Nedjar
Untitled, 1979-80
Cloth, glue and dye object
60 × 22 × 33 cm
Collection Irish Museum of Modern Art,
on loan from the Musgrave Kinley
Outsider Art Collection, Dublin

Margery Penfold
Despair II, 21 April 1936
Watercolour on paper
16.5 × 17.7 cm
Bethlem Art and Collections Trust

Roberto Pozo
Brick house and church, undated
Graphite on paper
23.1 × 30.6 cm
Bethlem Art and Collections Trust

Gilbert Price
Book, undated
Graphite on paper
20.3 × 12.8 cm
Bethlem Art and Collections Trust

Funnels, chimneys, vases, undated
Ink on tracing paper
20.2 × 27.6 cm
Bethlem Art and Collections Trust

G. R. X. D'Souza
The world of realism, 1956?
Graphite and watercolour on paper
19 × 28.2 cm
Bethlem Art and Collections Trust

Oswald Tschirtner
Madonna with Protective Coat, 1979
ink on paper
20.8 × 14.6 cm
Collection Irish Museum of Modern Art,
on loan from the Musgrave Kinley
Outsider Art Collection, Dublin (mg-0103)

Viele Menschen, 1977
14.3 × 10.3 cm
Collection Irish Museum of Modern Art,
on loan from the Musgrave Kinley
Outsider Art Collection, Dublin

Julian Trevelyan
Stage II, 1936
Pen and ink on paper
28.8 × 17.2 cm
Bethlem Art and Collections Trust

Stage I, 1936
Pen and ink on paper
17.6 × 22.8 cm
Bethlem Art and Collections Trust

Shafique Uddin
Untitled, undated
Gouache on paper
73 × 53.5 cm
Collection Irish Museum of Modern Art,
on loan from the Musgrave Kinley
Outsider Art Collection, Dublin

The Battle, 1986
Acrylic on canvas
122 × 153 cm
Collection Irish Museum of Modern Art,
on loan from the Musgrave Kinley
Outsider Art Collection, Dublin

Untitled, 1988
Watercolour on paper
58.5 × 84 cm
Collection Irish Museum of Modern Art,
on loan from the Musgrave Kinley
Outsider Art Collection, Dublin

Pascal Verbena
Leurrethiques, 1989
Silkscreen print, watercolour & text
36 × 26.3 cm
Collection Irish Museum of Modern Art,
on loan from the Musgrave Kinley
Outsider Art Collection, Dublin

Von Stropp
Manifesto, 1991
Ink on paper
62 × 47 cm
Bethlem Art and Collections Trust

Private C J Williams
Doodle, 3 May 1918
Graphite and ink on paper
24.8 × 19.8 cm
Bethlem Art and Collections Trust

Scottie Wilson
Untitled, undated
Pen, ink & crayon on paper
24 × 20 cm
Collection Irish Museum of Modern Art,
on loan from the Musgrave Kinley
Outsider Art Collection, Dublin (mg0101)

Untitled, undated
Pen, ink & crayon on paper
24 × 20 cm
Collection Irish Museum of Modern Art,
on loan from the Musgrave Kinley
Outsider Art Collection, Dublin

Agatha Wojciechowsky
Untitled, 1964
Watercolour and ink on paper
26 × 22.3 cm
Collection Irish Museum of Modern Art,
on loan from the Musgrave Kinley
Outsider Art Collection, Dublin

Adolf Wölfli
Untitled, undated
Pencil on paper
34 × 25 cm
Collection Irish Museum of Modern Art,
on loan from the Musgrave Kinley
Outsider Art Collection, Dublin

Anna Zemankova
Untitled, undated
Pencil, pen and embroidery silk on paper
62.3 × 44 cm
Collection Irish Museum of Modern Art,
on loan from the Musgrave Kinley
Outsider Art Collection, Dublin

This catalogue was published on occasion of the exhibition
Inner Worlds Outside, at the Whitechapel Gallery, London
April 28 – June 25, 2006

The exhibition is curated by Jon Thompson and Monika Kinley

Organised by
Anthony Spira, Curator, Whitechapel Gallery
Soledad Gutiérrez, Exhibitions Organiser, Whitechapel Gallery
Chris J. Aldgate, Gallery Manager, Whitechapel Gallery

Lenders
Irish Museum of Modern Art, Dublin
Musgrave Kinley Collection
London Borough of Newham Heritage Service
Bethlem Art and History Collections Trust
Galerie Jan Krugier, Ditesheim & Cie, Geneva
Grosvenor Gallery
Waddington Galleries Ltd.
Richard Nagy Ltd.
Martin Summers Fine Art
J. Todd Figi
And those who wish to remain anonymous.

Acknowledgements
Oliver Barker
Liana Braune
James Brett
Roger Manley
Catherine Marshall
Eimear Martin
Paul Pert
J. Michael Phillips
Richard Hyman Fine Art
Sean Sherman
Sotheby's London
Adam Lowe

Catalogue
Editor: Anthony Spira
Designer: O-SB Design
Proofreading: Anthony Spira, Candy Stobbs, Jon Thompson
Printing: St Ives Press, UK

Cover
77. Henry Darger
Untitled, c. 1940s–1960s
123. 'At Jennie Richee – Narrowly escape capture when attacked by Glandelinians
but the creatures 'gracefully' also show the Glandelinian the way out'. (verso).
Inside cover: 122. 'At Jennie Richee – After being shown how to escape from cavern
by their help they ask the creatures to display their wings which they do'. (recto)
Carbon tracing, collage, pencil and watercolour on paper
60.5 × 270.8 cm
Private collection

Photo Credits
Todd-White: cover, p.2, 4, 6,11,15–34 (top), 35–37(left), 39–41, 49 –51, 54, 56–59, 62–63,
65–71. Denis Mortell: p.4, 37 (right), 55, 62. Tate Archive: p.42. Roger Manley: p.43–47.
Waddington Galleries Ltd., p.12. Grosvenor Galleries: p.13 (top). Sotheby's: p.13.

Published by
Whitechapel Gallery
80–82 Whitechapel High Street
London E1 7QX, UK
T: +44 (0)20 7522 7888
F: +44 (0) 20 7377 1685
info@whitechapel.org
www.whitechapel.org

ISBN 0 85488 150 6

Whitechapel